Writing

Grades 9-12

How to Get

BETTER TEST SCORES

on Standardized Tests

Perfection Learning®

CREDITS

Senior Editor: Terry Ofner
Editor: Pegi Bevins
Art Director: Randy Messer
Designer: Deborah Lea Bell
Cover Illustration: Michael A. Aspengren

REVIEWERS

Denise M. Beeler
English Teacher
Bryan Station High School
Lexington, Kentucky

Joyce Vining Hill
Educational Consultant
Portage, Michigan

Robert A. Duncan
English Teacher
Carteret High School
Carteret, New Jersey

SCHOOL ACKNOWLEDGMENTS

Ankeny High School, Ankeny, Iowa
East High School, Des Moines, Iowa
Johnston High School, Johnston, Iowa
Madrid High School, Madrid, Iowa
Perry High School, Perry, Iowa
Waukee High School, Waukee, Iowa

©1998 Perfection Learning® Corporation
1000 North Second Avenue, P.O. Box 500, Logan, Iowa 51546-1099
Tel: 1-800-831-4190 • Fax: 1-712-644-2392
ISBN 0-7891-2347-9
Printed in the U.S.A.

TABLE OF CONTENTS

What Is the Purpose of an Essay Test?

As you know, there are many different ways to assess a student's knowledge. For example, you may have taken a standardized test that measured your basic skills or abilities. Perhaps you have done an assessment project at the end of a literature unit or given a graded speech in public speaking class. And you have probably taken your share of multiple choice and true/false tests. A standardized writing test is a little different from all of these.

A standardized writing test measures your ability to express your thoughts clearly and logically "on demand." In an on-demand situation, you must respond to a writing assignment, called a *prompt*, with no previous knowledge of what the topic might be.

A writing test may require you to compose a letter or write a report. Or a writing test might ask you to compose a letter to the editor or an article for your school newspaper. But more than likely, when you walk into a testing situation, you will be asked to write an essay. Essay writing is the focus of this book. (For information on other types of writing tests, see page 32.)

An essay is a piece of writing that expresses your thoughts on a particular topic. All essays include the following.

- **The introduction** is the first paragraph of the essay.
  The *introductory paragraph* introduces the topic and contains your central idea.

- **The body** consists of the paragraphs that follow the introduction.
  Each *body paragraph* contains a main point about your central idea and details to support that main point.

- **The conclusion** is the last paragraph of the essay.
  The *concluding paragraph* restates your central idea and sums up your thoughts.

To help remember the parts of an essay, look at the diagram below.

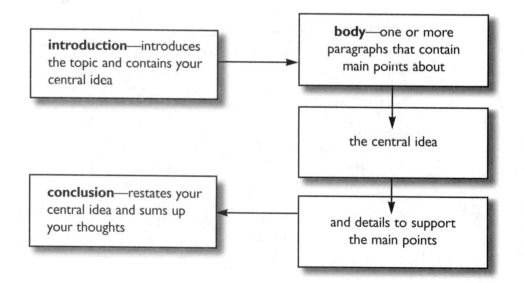

How Will My Essay Be Graded?

When you take a state or national test, your writing will normally be scored by one or more test evaluators, or readers. Test evaluators are trained to look for specific qualities in your writing. Here are the qualities a test evaluator might look for.

- focus—the degree to which the contents of your essay relate to the central idea
- organization—the order in which you present your ideas
- support—details you offer to back up your central idea
- conventions—the extent to which your writing conforms to the rules of the English language

Test readers often use rubrics to score student writing. A *rubric* is a set of specific qualities or standards. Listed below are the standards a test reader might use to evaluate your essay.

- The essay is well-organized, with a definite beginning, middle, and end.
- The essay has a clear central idea.
- The essay answers the prompt clearly and completely.
- The essay stays focused on the central idea throughout.
- The essay offers sufficient support for the central idea.
- The essay follows the rules of sentence structure and contains a variety of sentence lengths and styles.
- The essay follows the conventions, or rules, of punctuation, spelling, and grammar.

Why Do I Need This Book?

This book will show you how to get your thoughts down on paper quickly and in a logical and coherent manner. In addition, you will practice writing the most common types of essays. You will also be given a chance to see how other students responded to test prompts. Every few pages you will find handy test-taking tips and valuable writing strategies to make your essay the best it can be. And there's even a section on the most common problem areas in essay writing and how to avoid them. In short, this book will teach you how to get your essay right *the first time.*

How to
READ A PROMPT

A *prompt* is the assignment you receive on a writing test. A prompt provides you with instructions on what to write. It also determines the focus of your essay. However, the prompt does not always state the focus outright. It helps if you know how to read the prompt for clues to find your focus.

Noting Key Words and Phrases

Study the prompt from Maria's essay test. Notice the key words and phrases Maria underlined to help her determine the focus of her essay.

Prompt

Most children have a hero—a <u>role model</u> such as <u>a parent or teacher, a character from a movie or TV show, or possibly an outstanding athlete.</u> Think back to your childhood. Whom did you admire? <u>Choose a favorite hero from your childhood</u> and <u>explain why</u> he or she <u>appealed</u> to you.

The above prompt provides Maria with words or phrases that key her in to the kind of thinking her essay should demonstrate. The key phrase *explain why*, for example, tells Maria exactly what to do—explain why a certain childhood hero appealed to her. A thorough *explanation* makes something understandable by providing facts, examples, and/or reasons. Maria may want to include all of these kinds of details in her essay.

The prompt also gives suggestions about the actual subject of Maria's essay—a parent, teacher, movie or TV character, or athlete. In addition, it uses words Maria might consider using in her central idea—hero, role model, admire, appealed.

Read through the following prompt. Then go back and underline the key words or phrases that might be helpful to a writer.

READING A PROMPT

Step 1: Read through the entire prompt and decide what the general topic is.

Step 2: Read through the prompt a second time, underlining key words and phrases that narrow down the topic, for example, words like "explain" or "compare."

Step 3: Underline key words or phrases that provide suggestions for your writing.

Step 4: Look for key words or phrases you might be expected to use in your central idea.

Prompt

Some communities are considering establishing a curfew for teenagers to curb rising juvenile crime rates. Think about how a curfew would impact your life. Then write an essay that might convince your city council to vote either for or against a curfew.

As you progress through this book, use the steps in the Test-Taking Tip on this page to determine the focus of the prompts you encounter.

The EXPOSITORY ESSAY

When you explain the meaning of freedom, analyze the results of a science experiment, or compare two poems for English class, you are writing to explain. Writing to explain is also called *expository writing*. In an expository essay, you are expected to provide information or *explain* a topic.

Elements of an expository essay

- introductory paragraph
- one to three body paragraphs
- concluding paragraph

The *introductory paragraph* of an expository essay usually begins by introducing the topic and ends with the central idea. (See the Strategy of Good Writing sidebar on this page for ideas on introductions.) The *central idea* is a statement of fact or belief that you, as a writer, will support in your essay. For an expository essay, your central idea should contain two elements:

- the topic of the prompt
- your ideas, or main points, about the topic

Each *body paragraph* focuses on one of the main points of your central idea and offers details to support that main point.

The *concluding paragraph* restates your central idea. *Restate* in essay writing means to *reword* what you've said. Rewording your central idea provides variation for your readers. After restating your central idea, your concluding paragraph should sum up the thoughts you've expressed in the essay. A good concluding paragraph then ends with a strong thought that leaves your readers thinking about your ideas. Note: Your concluding paragraph signals the end of your essay. Therefore, avoid introducing new ideas in your concluding paragraph.

Words you might find in an expository essay prompt

analyze	contrast	respond to
clarify	define	propose
classify	discuss	summarize
compare	explain	trace

Strategy OF GOOD WRITING

GETTING YOUR READERS' ATTENTION

A good writer opens an essay with a "hook" that grabs readers' attention. You may have some strategies of your own for hooking readers. If not, below are several types of hooks that work for most papers.

- **Surprise your readers.** Shock them with a statistic or fact, or provide them with a startling description.

- **Entertain them.** Tell your audience a riveting story or an amusing anecdote.

- **Offer them a challenge.** Ask your readers a question or invite them to solve a problem. You might even issue them a command.

- **Make your readers think.** Begin with a thought-provoking question, statement, quotation, or saying.

continued

Below is the expository essay prompt Seth was given on a writing test.

Prompt

Students often complain about their school lunch program. <u>Think about what you don't like about your lunch program.</u> <u>Propose ways</u> that <u>lunchtime</u> at your school <u>could be made more enjoyable for students</u>.

Getting Started

Seth began by underlining key words and phrases. His next step was to organize his ideas about improving the school lunch program. Look at the web diagram below that he created. Notice that he placed the topic of the diagram—ways to improve lunchtime at his school—in the center and then arranged his ideas around it.

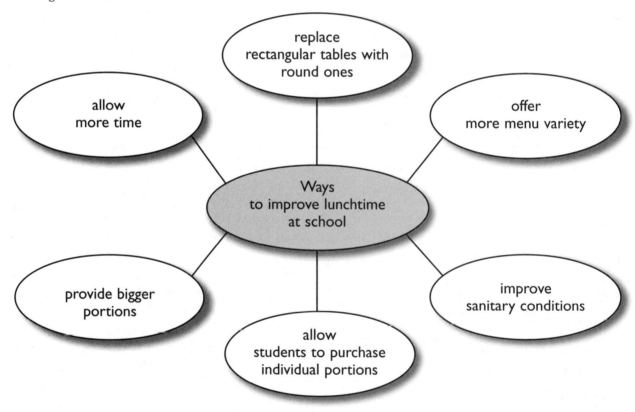

Look for evidence of the preplanning Seth did as you read his essay beginning on the next page.

SETH'S ESSAY

Every day at 11:30, the scene is the same. With expectations of good food and conversation, students hurry through the halls and pour into the cafeteria, only to be greeted by long lines, skimpy portions, and the disgusting, but real, possibility of finding a hair in their food! Ask students if they are getting their money's worth, and they will probably answer with a resounding, "No way!" However, with just a few changes, lunchtime could be a more satisfying experience for everyone. The school lunch program could be improved by extending the lunch period, offering bigger portions, and enforcing stricter sanitary standards.

If the lunch program is to improve, students must be given more time to eat. As the schedule is set up now, lunchtime provides more stress than pleasure for students. To illustrate, fourth period bell rings at 11:30. Students must be to fifth period by 11:55 or be considered tardy. During those 25 minutes, students must go to their lockers, hit the restroom if necessary, stand in line in the lunchroom (10 minutes minimum), find a place to sit, eat their food, and make their way to fifth period class. Extending the lunch period by a mere five minutes would allow students a little leeway and cut down immensely on their stress. And it would allow students to actually chew rather than gulp their food. In conclusion, a longer lunch period is a must if students are to graduate from high school without the beginnings of stress-related heart disease!

Besides getting more time to eat, students should also be given bigger portions of food. One hot dog, a few fries, and 12 green beans is not enough to get most students through another four hours of classes. Bigger portions of food would give students enough energy to make it through the rest of the day.

Additional time and bigger portions will only be relevant, however, if sanitary conditions are improved. For example, often the tables and the floor are caked with remnants of yesterday's menu. In addition, food

continued

Examining SETH'S ESSAY

- Does Seth's introductory paragraph grab your attention? Why or why not?

- Locate Seth's central idea. Does it clearly reflect the topic of the prompt and Seth's ideas about the topic?

- Are the main ideas of Seth's body paragraphs clearly stated?

- Are the details Seth offers in his body paragraphs relevant to the topic?

- Which body paragraph is lacking in support? What kinds of details might Seth have added to this paragraph?

Examining
SETH'S ESSAY

- Does Seth restate his central idea in the concluding paragraph?

- Does he sum up his thoughts about the topic?

- How effective is Seth's ending?

is left out uncovered where it is exposed to flies and the sneezes of anyone who walks by. Students have reported finding hair, fingernails, and even Band-Aids in their food. One wonders where the health department is these days. To remedy this, the cooks should be required to wear hair nets and plastic gloves, the janitors should do a more thorough clean-up of the cafeteria, and steps should be taken to protect food at all times. After all, students should not have to be afraid of what they might find when they sit down to lunch.

In conclusion, the school lunch program needs to be overhauled. This could be accomplished by giving students more time to eat, serving them bigger portions of food, and providing them with a cleaner environment to eat in. Mealtime is supposed to be a pleasant experience for all. As it stands now, the only ones who enjoy it are the flies!

On Your Own

Now it's your turn to write an expository essay. Read the prompt below.

Prompt

> Irish poet Oscar Wilde (1854–1900) once said, "The best way to make children good is to make them happy." In an essay, respond to Wilde's approach to child-rearing.

Begin by underlining key words and phrases in the prompt. then use the blank organizer below to generate ideas about Wilde's approach to child-rearing. Refer to the organizer as you write your essay. (See the Test-Taking Tip on this page for help in narrowing down your ideas.)

When you finish writing, apply the rubric on the next page to your essay. Fill in the appropriate circle for each standard in the Score column (*1* is the lowest; *5* is the highest).

Time Allowed

minutes

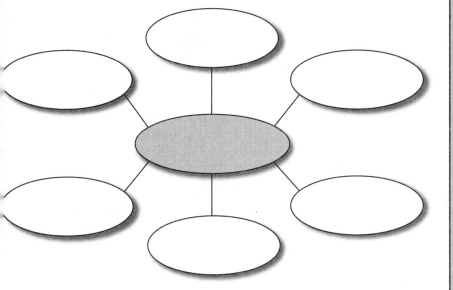

Test-Taking
TIP

NARROWING DOWN YOUR IDEAS QUICKLY

When narrowing down your ideas into a workable central idea, consider the following.

- Select the ideas you know most about. They will be easiest to support.

- Select the most important ideas. Weak support makes for a weak paper.

- Select the ideas your audience will be familiar with. Readers will find it easier to identify with ideas they know something about. Also, by presenting your readers with familiar ideas, you can avoid lengthy and time-consuming explanations.

continued

Rubric	Score (*1* is the lowest; *5* is the highest)
My introductory paragraph grabs readers' attention.	① ② ③ ④ ⑤
My introductory paragraph includes a clear central idea that reflects the topic of the prompt and the main points of the essay.	① ② ③ ④ ⑤
Each of my body paragraphs focuses on a main point of the central idea.	① ② ③ ④ ⑤
Each of my body paragraphs offers a sufficient number of relevant details to support the main point.	① ② ③ ④ ⑤
My concluding paragraph sums up my ideas and restates my central idea.	① ② ③ ④ ⑤
My essay ends with a strong thought that will leave my readers thinking about my ideas.	① ② ③ ④ ⑤
My essay follows the conventions of written English.	① ② ③ ④ ⑤

Consider This

1. Based on the rubric, what are your strengths in expository essay writing? What are your weaknesses?

2. If you were the test reader, do you think you would find your essay interesting? If not, what could you do to make your essay more appealing?

The PERSUASIVE ESSAY

When you write a speech that tells why you should be elected class president or when you try to convince your parents to extend your curfew time, you are being persuasive. In a *persuasive essay*, you are expected to state an opinion about a controversial issue and then try to *persuade* your readers to agree with your opinion. A *controversial issue* is any issue that has two or more sides.

Elements of a persuasive essay

- introductory paragraph
- three to five body paragraphs
- concluding paragraph

The *introductory paragraph* of a persuasive essay usually begins by introducing the issue and ends with the central idea. The central idea is a statement of your opinion on the issue.

Each body paragraph should focus on your central idea. There are two types of *body paragraphs* in a persuasive essay, pro and con.

- *Pro paragraphs* focus on arguments that support your opinion. For example, suppose your school is considering implementing a policy that requires students to wear uniforms to school. If you are writing an essay in favor of such a policy, any argument you use to support your opinion is a pro. If, on the other hand, your friend is writing an essay that disagrees with such a policy, any argument she includes that is against students being forced to wear uniforms is a pro. Remember: pro paragraphs support the writer's opinion, whether he or she is for or against an idea.

- *Con paragraphs* focus on arguments against your opinion. Including con paragraphs draws your readers into your essay and indicates to them that you are a well-informed person who recognizes that there are two sides to the issue you are addressing. (See the Strategy of Good Writing sidebar on this page for ideas on how to organize your body paragraphs.)

Strategy OF GOOD WRITING

ORGANIZING PROS AND CONS

When organizing your persuasive essay, keep the following in mind.

- A good writer places a con paragraph at the beginning of the body of the essay. This strategy establishes "common ground" with readers from the beginning and makes them more likely to continue reading.

- A good writer places the strongest pro paragraph at the end of the body of the essay. This strategy builds support gradually and leaves readers with the strongest argument in mind.

Choose one of the following organizational strategies for your body paragraphs.

Strategy 1	Strategy 2
con	con
con	pro
pro	con
pro	pro
strongest pro	strongest pro

continued

The *concluding paragraph* begins with a restatement, or rewording, of your central idea. Rewording your central idea provides variation for your readers. An effective concluding paragraph also reminds readers of your pros. Your concluding paragraph should also end with a strong thought that leaves your readers thinking about your ideas.

Words you might find in a persuasive essay prompt		
agree, disagree	debate	position
argue, argument	issue	should, should not
consider	opinion	stance
controversy, controversial	oppose	support
convince	persuade	viewpoint

Below is an example of a persuasive essay prompt that Stacie was given on a writing test. Note: Your concluding paragraph signals the end of your essay. Therefore, avoid introducing new ideas in your concluding paragraph.

Prompt

Some school districts are voting on whether <u>schools should be kept open year around.</u> Students would attend school the same number of days, but the <u>long summer vacation would be broken up</u> into two- to three-week <u>breaks</u> interspersed <u>throughout the year.</u> Consider the <u>pros and cons of year-round school.</u> In a <u>persuasive essay,</u> attempt to <u>convince your local school board to either accept or reject the idea of year-round school.</u>

Getting Started

Stacie began by underlining key words and phrases in the prompt. Next she decided whether she was for or against year-round school and organized her ideas about the issue using the chart to the right. Notice that she placed her position—that she is against year-round school—at the top of the chart and then listed her pros and cons in separate columns. Reminder: Since Stacie is against year-round school, any argument against year-round school is a pro. Any argument in favor of year-round schooling is a con—it's against Stacie's opinion.

As you examine Stacie's essay on the next page, respond to the questions in the column beside it..

Look for evidence of the preplanning Stacie did as you read her essay beginning on the next page.

Issue: year-round school
My position: against

Pros	Cons
vacation schedule would conflict with schedules of relatives and friends who have traditional summer vacation	long summer vacations can become boring for many students
would make it hard for students to have the equivalent of a summer job	teachers have to spend time reteaching in the fall
summer weather is made for vacations; other times of the year the weather is not so dependable	summer vacations were originally set up for an agriculturally-based society; no longer the case
tradition: it's always been done this way, why change?	vacations can be taken in off-seasons, which can be beneficial (less expensive, less crowded, etc.)
three-month vacation gives students a much-needed break	

STACIE'S ESSAY

Kids and summer just naturally go together. Endless days of warmth and sun, baseball, swimming in the local pool, going barefoot—a kid can really only have these experiences in the summer. How can anyone imagine spending such a magical time sitting in a school building? School can take place in any kind of weather; summer can only "take place" in summer. In the interests of the kids of this school district, the local school board should retain the current school-year schedule.

Granted, long summer vacations can become boring for some kids. The thrill of just being out of school can occupy the first couple of weeks, but after the newness wears off, boredom often sets in. For the child who isn't old enough to get a job or drive a car, this is especially true. In addition, many kids lose touch with their school chums during the summer and can actually end up spending a lot of time alone. Time alone often results in time in the house watching television and playing video games, not exactly what summer weather was made for. Shorter breaks provided by a year-round school schedule would probably be more enjoyable to students who have a tendency to become bored.

On the other hand, the long summer break enables students who can't work while school is in session to make money during the summer. Summer jobs have traditionally been an important source of income for teenagers. Summer jobs allow teens to buy the "extras" they want, such as stereos and designer clothing. They also give students a means of saving for college. Conversely, a year-round school schedule would break the three-month vacation into several shorter ones. Few employers would allow a student to work three weeks, quit for eight, and then come back to work for three more.

Still, some would argue that as a result of long summer vacations, teachers are forced to spend too much time in the fall "reteaching." Three months is a long time for students to remember some concepts,

Examining STACIE'S ESSAY

- Does Stacie's introductory paragraph grab your attention? Why or why not?

- Locate Stacie's central idea. Is her opinion on year-round school clearly stated?

- Locate Stacie's con paragraphs. Are the details Stacie offers in these paragraphs relevant to the topic?

continued

Examining
STACIE'S ESSAY

- Locate Stacie's pro paragraphs. Are the details she offers in these paragraphs relevant to the topic?

- Which pro paragraph is lacking in support? What kinds of details might Stacie have added to this paragraph?

- Which organizational strategy did Stacy use for her essay?

- Does Stacy restate her central idea in the concluding paragraph?

- Does she remind her readers of her pros in this paragraph?

especially those they don't use very often. The shorter breaks provided by a year-round school schedule might prevent such concepts from "slipping away." This, in turn, could allow teachers to basically pick up where they left off two to three weeks earlier instead of backtracking after a three months' absence. Since reteaching delays new learning, some feel that year-round school might be something to consider.

While reteaching is certainly an issue, traditional summer vacations give kids a much-needed break from school. Nine months of getting up early, gulping breakfast, running to catch the bus, taking tests, and doing homework can take its toll on a kid, both mentally and physically. This is not to mention all the other stress factors many students have today: good things like competitive sports and music lessons and not-so-good things like peer pressure, divorce, drugs, and violence. Just as adults need an extended break from their jobs, so do kids need an extended break from their schooling.

Most importantly, the current school-year schedule should be retained because it is deeply rooted in the traditions of this society. For the most part, students in the United States have always gone to school in September and gotten out in June, and much of society reflects this. One can't argue with a tradition that has lasted as long as this one.

Clearly then, the local school board should reject the idea of year-round school. To repeat, the traditional schedule allows students to hold down summer jobs. Also, the long summer vacation provides students with a much-needed break from the pressures of school. Most importantly, the current schedule is an accepted tradition in this society. The year-round pressures of adulthood are going to be part of kids' lives soon enough. Kids should be allowed to just be kids—at least for three months out of the year.

On Your Own

Now it's your turn to write a persuasive essay. Read the prompt below.

Prompt

> With the recent rise of substance abuse among teenagers, school officials are devising ways to curb the distribution and availability of drugs in schools. One of these methods involves routine searches of students' lockers. Consider the arguments for and against this issue. Then write a persuasive essay that presents your opinion on the idea of routine searches of students' lockers.

Begin by locating key words and phrases in the prompt. Then decide whether you are for or against routine searches of students' lockers. Use the blank organizer below to generate your pros and cons. Be sure to refer to the organizer as you write your essay. (See the Test-Taking Tip on this page if you need help selecting your pros and cons.)

When you finish writing, apply the rubric on the next page to your essay. Fill in the appropriate circle for each standard in the Score column (*1* is the lowest; *5* is the highest).

Time Allowed

minutes

Test-Taking
TIP

SELECTING YOUR PROS AND CONS QUICKLY

When trying to decide which pros and cons to include in your essay, consider the following.

- Include the strongest arguments in favor of your opinion in your pro paragraphs. Normally the strongest arguments will be easiest to support.

- Include the strongest arguments against your opinion in your con paragraphs. Your reader will be impressed that you're not afraid to acknowledge these opposing ideas.

Issue:	
My Position:	
Pros	**Cons**

continued

Rubric	Score (*1* is the lowest; *5* is the highest)
My introductory paragraph grabs the readers' attention.	① ② ③ ④ ⑤
My introductory paragraph includes a clear central idea that reflects my opinion of the issue.	① ② ③ ④ ⑤
My con paragraph(s) contain a sufficient number of relevant details.	① ② ③ ④ ⑤
My pro paragraphs contain a sufficient number of details that support the arguments in favor of my position.	① ② ③ ④ ⑤
My concluding paragraph restates my central idea and reminds readers of my pros.	① ② ③ ④ ⑤
My essay ends with a strong thought that will leave my readers thinking about my ideas.	① ② ③ ④ ⑤
My essay follows the conventions of written English.	① ② ③ ④ ⑤

Consider This

1. Based on the rubric, what are your strengths in persuasive essay writing? What are your weaknesses?

2. If you were a test reader, do you think you would be persuaded to agree with your opinion? If not, what could you do to make your essay more convincing?

The NARRATIVE ESSAY

When you tell your friends about something that happened to you or when you write a new ending for a story you have read in English class, you are narrating. On a *narrative essay* test, you are expected to tell the story of a significant event from your life.

Elements of a narrative essay

- introductory paragraph
- one or more body paragraphs
- concluding paragraph

A narrative usually follows a typical plot line. *A plot line* consists of

- The *introduction* introduces the characters and setting, and provides background information.
- The *rising action* consists of the events that lead to the point of greatest interest in the plot.
- The *climax* is the point of greatest interest in the plot.
- The *falling action* consists of the events that follow the climax and lead to the resolution.
- The *resolution* is the final outcome that ties up any loose ends in the story.

Read on to see how you might plan your narrative essay using a plot diagram.

The *introductory paragraph* of a narrative essay serves as the introduction for your essay. This first paragraph sets the scene by introducing the characters and giving details about the setting of your event. It is also the logical place to provide any background information readers might need to better understand the essay. The introductory paragraph should include a central idea. (See the Test-Taking Tip on this page.)

The *body* of a narrative essay can consist of any number of paragraphs. Some stories may require only one or two paragraphs. Others may require several. The rising action, the climax, and the falling action should all be included in the body paragraphs of a narrative essay. More than likely you will want to organize the events in the body of your narrative essay in chronological order.

The *concluding paragraph* provides the resolution, or ending, for the story. The concluding paragraph also offers any reflections or

Test-Taking TIP

CENTRAL IDEA— NARRATIVE ESSAY

The central idea of a narrative essay can be a direct statement of what your essay will focus on.

Example: *An event that forced me to grow up quickly was the flood that occurred last spring.*

Or the central idea might simply be indicated in the introductory information.

Example: *I used to have a photograph album filled with pictures of all the people who mattered to me. I kept it in the bottom drawer of my dresser. Whenever I was bored, I'd take it out and look at it. But my bedroom is in the basement of our house, and last spring the creek in back of our property flooded. By the time it was over, our basement had two feet of water in it. I lost that album, along with a lot of other precious belongings, in the flood that year. I also lost part of my childhood.*

The important thing to remember is that by the time your readers finish the first paragraph, they should be able to identify the focus of your paper.

continued

thoughts you might have about the event. For example, you might explain what the experience taught you or how it changed you. A good concluding paragraph ends with a strong thought that leaves your readers thinking about what you have written. Note: Your concluding paragraph signals the end of your essay. Therefore, avoid introducing new ideas in your concluding paragraph.

Below is a plot diagram for a narrative essay you might write.

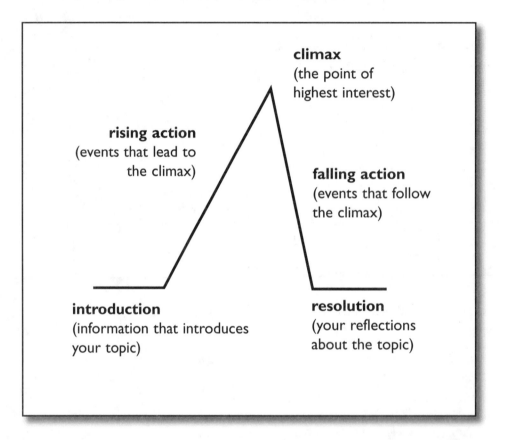

climax
(the point of highest interest)

rising action
(events that lead to the climax)

falling action
(events that follow the climax)

introduction
(information that introduces your topic)

resolution
(your reflections about the topic)

Words you might find in a narrative essay prompt

event	relate
experience	remember
incident	story
narrate	tell
recall	time
recount	

Below is an example of a narrative essay prompt that Michaelah was given on a writing test.

Prompt

<u>Nature</u> can be a <u>terrifying</u> force. In a <u>narrative essay</u>, <u>relate a time when you struggled against an element of nature.</u>

Getting Started

Michaelah began by underlining key words and phrases in the prompt. Then she mapped out her story. Look at the plot diagram that she created.

climax
- realized we were out too far
- headed back to shore
- waves were hard to swim through
- struggled against undertow
- thought I was going to die

rising action
- started jumping waves
- undertow was strong
- swam out farther
- Laura's dad joined us

introduction
- vacationing with Laura and her family
- location of Mare's Head
- definition of undertow

falling action
- made it back to shore
- swore I'd never leave land again

resolution
- back in the water later that day
- learned how dangerous undertow can be

As you read Michaelah's essay beginning on the next page, look for evidence of the preplanning she did.

continued

MICHAELAH'S ESSAY

Examining MICHAELAH'S ESSAY

- Does Michaelah's introductory paragraph grab your attention? Why or why not?

- Does Michaelah introduce the characters and give details about the setting of her story in her introductory paragraph?

- Does Michaelah's introductory paragraph provide any background knowledge necessary to understand the essay?

- Locate Michaelah's central idea.

- Label the rising action in the body paragraphs. Do the events seem to be organized in chronological order?

The movie <u>Jaws</u> has done a lot toward causing people to fear the ocean. Images of circling shark fins and feeding frenzies are enough to make anyone stay out of the water. But as far as I am concerned, the scariest "creature" that exists in the ocean is the undertow. An undertow is an underlying current that moves opposite the direction that the waves move. I learned more than I wanted to know about the undertow when I was ten years old. My family and I were on vacation with my best friend, Laura, and her family in Mare's Head. Mare's Head is a small town on one of the Outer Isles, a group of small islands off the coast. On one side of Mare's Head is the ocean, and on the other is the sound. The first day we were there, Laura and I headed into the water for a swim, and that's when I realized just how scary the undertow can be.

As we ran down the beach, I remember thinking what a great day it was going to be. The weather was a perfect 92 degrees, the water was clear and warm, and the waves were killers—just the way I like them. I have always been quite daring in the water, and I could hardly wait to start jumping those big waves. We went out about 20 feet, to the point where the water covered our chests. We wanted to go out farther, but our parents would not let us because the undertow was very strong that day. We were disappointed, but we knew they were right. Like an invisible force beneath the water, the undertow tugged at our legs, at times almost knocking us down. Laura and I jumped on the first big wave and were immediately carried back toward the shore a few feet. Then we swam out again and waited for the next wave. After we had done this a few times, we started swimming a little farther out into the water because we were being washed in so far every time. That is when Laura's dad joined us. I guess he thought we would be safer with an adult.

After a few minutes, Laura's dad realized we were out way too far and told us it was time to go back to the beach. Easier said than done. The waves were so

big by that time that it was really hard to get through them. That's when the undertow started pulling us away from the shore. When you are in trouble with the undertow, you swim at an angle. We put all our strength into it but could feel the force of the undertow resisting us. It was very tiring. The waves kept crashing into us from above, and the undertow kept dragging at us from below. As I struggled, my arms and legs began to feel like rubber, and I was afraid I wasn't going to be able to make it. I kept spitting out huge mouthfuls of salt water and repeating to myself, "I'm going to die. I'm going to die."

It had only taken us a minute to swim out. It took us 20 minutes to get back to shore. When we finally reached the beach, I threw myself down on the sand and lay there thinking, "I love land. I love land. I'm never going to leave it again."

Of course, I did leave the land again. In fact, before the day was over, we were back in the water jumping waves. But this time we stayed a lot closer to the shore. You might think this experience would have left me terrified of the ocean. Actually, it didn't. I love the ocean and I always will. But it did make me realize how dangerous the undertow can be and how much respect it deserves. I might even go so far as to say I'll take sharks anytime. At least sharks you can see.

Examining MICHAELAH'S ESSAY

- Now label the climax. Does the rising action lead logically to the climax?

- Does the concluding paragraph provide a resolution for the story?

- Does Michaelah include any insight she has gained from the event?

- How effective is Michaelah's ending?

continued

On Your Own

Now it's your turn to write a narrative essay. Read the prompt below.

Prompt

Someone once said that the most predictable thing about life is that it is unpredictable. In a narrative essay, tell about an event in your life that didn't work out the way you predicted.

Begin by locating key words and phrases in the prompt. Then use the blank organizer below to map out your story. Remember to refer to the organizer as you write your essay.

When you finish writing, apply the rubric on the next page to your essay. Fill in the appropriate circle for each standard in the Score column (*1* is the lowest; *5* is the highest).

Time Allowed

minutes

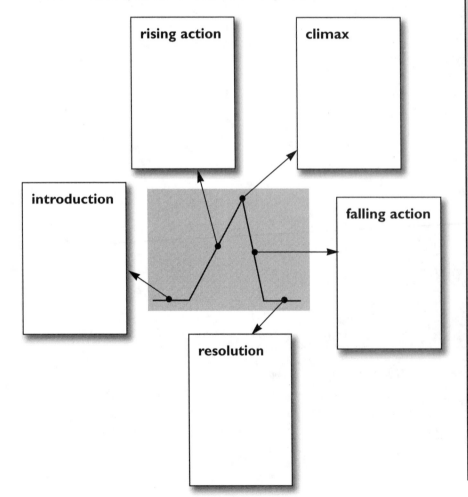

rising action

climax

introduction

falling action

resolution

Strategy
OF GOOD WRITING

MAKING YOUR NARRATION INTERESTING

Young writers often overuse the word "then" in recounting a series of events. Look at the following example.

"I decided to go to bed. Then I heard a noise and stopped. Then I turned around slowly. I couldn't believe my eyes. Then a scream arose from the depths of me. Then I fainted."

A good writer uses a variety of methods to move from one event to another. Read the following revision of the above narration.

"On my way to bed, I heard a noise. When I turned around, I couldn't believe what I saw. A scream arose from the depths of me. Then I fainted."

Overuse of any word or phrase can become tiring for readers Remember, variety is the key to interesting writing.

Rubric	Score (*1* is the lowest; *5* is the highest)
My introductory paragraph introduces the characters and gives details about the setting.	① ② ③ ④ ⑤
My introductory paragraph provides any background knowledge necessary for readers to understand the essay.	① ② ③ ④ ⑤
My introductory paragraph indicates what the focus of the essay will be.	① ② ③ ④ ⑤
My body paragraphs contain the rising action, the climax, and the falling action of the story.	① ② ③ ④ ⑤
The events of my story are organized in chronological order.	① ② ③ ④ ⑤
My concluding paragraph provides a resolution or ending for my story.	① ② ③ ④ ⑤
My concluding paragraph provides insight into the event.	① ② ③ ④ ⑤
My essay ends with a strong thought that will leave my readers thinking about my story.	① ② ③ ④ ⑤
My essay follows the conventions of written English.	① ② ③ ④ ⑤

Consider This

1. Based on the rubric, what are your strengths in narrative essay writing? What are your weaknesses?

2. If you were a test reader, do you think you would easily be able to follow the "plot line" of this essay? Do you think you would find this story interesting? If not, what could you do to make your essay easier to follow and/or more interesting?

Strategy
OF GOOD WRITING

INCLUDE
SENSORY DETAILS

A good writer provides readers with sensory details. Sensory details are details that awaken the reader's senses. Such details are particularly important in descriptive writing. They help readers experience the writer's personal reactions and feelings. For example, "Leaves rose into tiny whirlwinds, old newspapers tumbled wildly down the street, and every flag stood at attention" provides readers with a much clearer picture than "It was windy outside."

Remember, the most effective writing is writing that the reader can experience. To make your writing more effective, includes lots of sensory details. (For additional help on creating effective sensory details, see page 49.)

The
DESCRIPTIVE ESSAY

When you write your feelings in a journal or when you try to explain to your friend what your favorite group's music is like, you are being descriptive. In a *descriptive essay*, you are expected to describe a person, an object, or an event.

Elements of a descriptive essay

- introductory paragraph
- one or more body paragraphs
- concluding paragraph

The introductory paragraph of a descriptive essay introduces the topic of the essay. The introductory paragraph should also include the central idea. Your central idea should contain two elements:

- the topic
- a general impression about the topic

The body of a descriptive essay can consist of any number of paragraphs. Some topics may require three or four paragraphs to describe. Others may require only one or two. The body paragraphs of your descriptive essay should include all the details needed to describe your topic. (See the Strategy of Good Writing sidebar on this page.) These details should be organized in a logical manner: top to bottom, for example, front to back, or beginning to end.

The concluding paragraph should restate your central idea using different wording. Rewording your central idea provides variation for your readers. A good concluding paragraph also ends with a strong thought that leaves your readers thinking about your ideas. Note: Your concluding paragraph signals the end of your essay. Therefore, avoid introducing new ideas in your concluding paragraph.

Words you might find in a descriptive essay prompt

convey	picture
depict	portray
describe, description	senses, sensory
express	visualize

Below is an example of a descriptive essay prompt K.C. was given on a writing test.

Prompt

Most people have an item they treasure: a piece of clothing, a souvenir from a special time, a book, etc. In an essay, describe one of your favorite possessions and tell why you treasure it.

Getting Started

K.C. began by underlining key words and phrases in the prompt. Then he organized his ideas and details about the item he selected—his baseball glove. Look at the organizer that he created.

BASEBALL GLOVE

why I treasure memories

smell of leather brings back the day I got the glove

autograph on back brings back the Cubs game Grandpa took me to

gift from my Grandfather

spent the day oiling it

Grandpa convinced me to ask for Sandburg's autograph

Ryne told me I had a nice glove

glove helps me deal with Grandpa's death

As you read K.C.'s essay beginning on the next page, look for evidence of the preplanning he did.

continued

K.C.'s Essay

Examining K.C.'s Essay

- Does K.C.'s introductory paragraph "grab" your attention? Why or why not?

- Locate K.C.'s central idea. Does it contain a general impression about the topic?

- Do K.C.'s body paragraphs support the central idea?

- Underline the sensory details in this paragraph. Are there any others K.C. might have included?

My love affair with baseball began when I was about five years old. My grandfather, a devoted baseball fan, would take me into the front yard and pitch a plastic ball to me. I would stand with my Cubs hat on backward, hold the oversized red plastic bat in my hands, and swing away. As I remember, I spent more time retrieving the ball from in back of me than Grandpa did from in front. Then when I was seven, my grandfather bought me my first baseball glove. Our game switched to catch. Again, I did a lot more retrieving than anything. But we had fun, and I think Grandpa knew that he was instilling in me a love for the game. Last year my grandpa died. He was 82, and I miss him a lot, particularly on warm spring days. Luckily he left me with a passion for baseball that will last a lifetime. But the best thing he left me with was a baseball glove full of memories.

If I hold my baseball glove up to my face and sniff, I am taken back to the day I got the glove. One morning Grandpa called to tell me he had a surprise for me and he was coming right over. I waited anxiously on the back steps. When Grandpa's Buick pulled into the driveway, I raced over to it.

"Here you go, buddy boy," Grandpa said as he handed me a sack. I could smell the leather before I even opened the bag. For an instant, I was disappointed because I thought he had bought me a pair of shoes. But then I pulled the glove out and couldn't believe it—it was so big! One finger seemed big enough to hold my whole hand!

"This is a man's glove," Grandpa said. "If you're going to get serious about this game, you've got to have a serious glove." We spent the next hour oiling the glove because Grandpa said the leather would crack if we didn't. As Grandpa massaged the oil into the glove, it crackled and creaked and filled the air with the rich smell of new leather. I've used this glove for almost ten years now. It might not be new anymore, but the smell of leather is still there and never fails to bring back that day.

The back of my glove is autographed by Ryne Sandburg, second baseman for the Chicago Cubs. Every time I look at that autograph, I remember the first and only time I've been to a major league baseball game. And it was also the first and only time my parents allowed me to miss school when I wasn't sick. The Cubs were playing the Yankees, and Grandpa had gotten great seats by the first base line. We arrived an hour early, "just in case the players are signing," he said. The stadium was huge, with rows and rows of seats and brightly colored flags flying everywhere. As we were taking our seats, the players entered the field. "Now's your chance," Grandpa said, nudging me. "Run up there!"

He gave me a marker pen, and I grabbed my glove and ran to the front of the grandstands. Since it was a weekday, there were very few other kids there. Ryne Sandburg was just passing by. At first I just stood and stared. I couldn't believe I was actually seeing him in person. Finally, I gathered up my courage and called out, "Hey, Mr. Sandburg, can I have your autograph—please?"

I had heard that lots of times players won't sign before a game, and I half-expected him to ignore me, but that day Ryne looked around, saw that there weren't a million other kids waiting, and said, "Sure, kid." He came over and I handed him my glove and the pen. "Nice glove," he said and signed his name.

As I headed back to my seat, I could see Grandpa smiling like crazy. I could tell that he was as happy for me as I was for myself. It turned out to be a lousy game; the Cubs lost 13–3, but I don't remember being disappointed or bored. All I remember is Ryne Sandburg saying I had a nice glove.

I treasure the memories my baseball glove provides me. Somehow it makes it easier to deal with the fact that Grandpa is not around anymore. But as the saying goes, memories mare forever. And I've got the glove to prove it.

Examining K.C.'s Essay

- Underline the sensory details in this essay. Are there any others K.C. might have included?

- How effective is K.C.'s ending?

continued

On Your Own

Now it's your turn to write a descriptive essay. Read the prompt below.

Prompt

Imagine that you and your family want to sell your house. You've been contacted by someone from out of town who saw your ad in the newspaper. The potential buyer would like a description of your house before she makes the decision to travel to your town to see it. Each of your family members has decided to describe his or her favorite part of the house.

Describe your favorite room or area of your house so that the potential buyer gets a clear picture of it.

Begin by locating Key words and phrases in the prompt. Then use the blank organizer below to generate ideas and details about your favorite room or area of your house. Refer to the organizer as you write your essay.

When you finish writing, apply the rubric on the next page to your essay. Fill in the appropriate circle for each standard in the Score column (*1* is the lowest; *5* is the highest).

Time Allowed

minutes

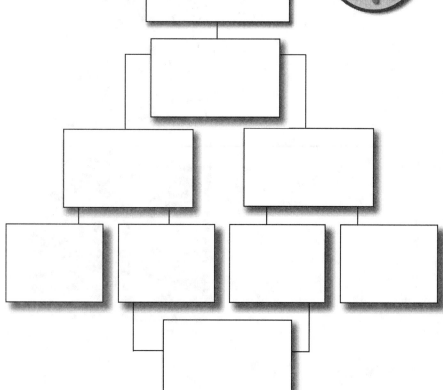

Rubric	Score (*1* is the lowest; *5* is the highest)
My introductory paragraph grabs readers' attention.	① ② ③ ④ ⑤
My introductory paragraph includes a clear central idea.	① ② ③ ④ ⑤
My body paragraphs include sufficient sensory details to provide my reader with a true sense of my topic.	① ② ③ ④ ⑤
My details are presented in a logical order.	① ② ③ ④ ⑤
My concluding paragraph restates my central idea.	① ② ③ ④ ⑤
My essay ends with a strong thought that will leave my readers thinking about my ideas.	① ② ③ ④ ⑤
My essay follows the conventions of written English.	① ② ③ ④ ⑤

Consider This

1. Based on the rubric, what are your strengths in descriptive essay writing? What are your weaknesses?

2. If you were the test reader, do you think you would get a clear picture of the topic of this essay? Do you think you would find the descriptions interesting? If not, what could you do as the writer to make your essay more clear and interesting?

Other Types
OF WRITING TESTS

The most common type of writing test will ask you to write an essay such as those discussed earlier. But some tests require different forms of writing. Some of these other types of writing tests are listed below.

---

friendly letter
an informal letter to a friend, relative, or acquaintance

---

business letter
a formal letter to an employer, a businessperson, a lawmaker, or another professional

---

letter to the editor
a formal letter suitable for publishing in a newspaper. Normally the letter expresses an opinion on an issue.

---

report
an informal report based on a list of facts provided

Since most writing is either expository, persuasive, narrative, or descriptive, you should be able to apply the skills you've already learned in essay writing to these types of assignments. This chapter will show you how. For practice in other types of writing tests, see page 38.

FRIENDLY LETTER

Depending on the prompt, you could be asked to do any of the four types of writing in a friendly letter.

Read the prompt to the right. Then notice the elements of a persuasive essay in the friendly letter below.

Prompt

Your favorite cousin is considering dropping out of school. In a friendly letter, persuade your cousin to complete his or her senior year.

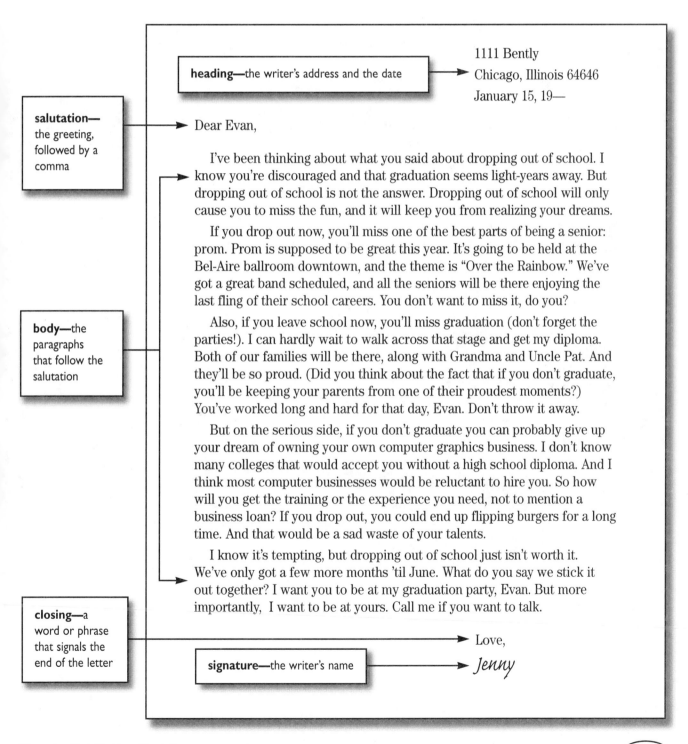

heading—the writer's address and the date

1111 Bently
Chicago, Illinois 64646
January 15, 19—

salutation—the greeting, followed by a comma

Dear Evan,

I've been thinking about what you said about dropping out of school. I know you're discouraged and that graduation seems light-years away. But dropping out of school is not the answer. Dropping out of school will only cause you to miss the fun, and it will keep you from realizing your dreams.

If you drop out now, you'll miss one of the best parts of being a senior: prom. Prom is supposed to be great this year. It's going to be held at the Bel-Aire ballroom downtown, and the theme is "Over the Rainbow." We've got a great band scheduled, and all the seniors will be there enjoying the last fling of their school careers. You don't want to miss it, do you?

Also, if you leave school now, you'll miss graduation (don't forget the parties!). I can hardly wait to walk across that stage and get my diploma. Both of our families will be there, along with Grandma and Uncle Pat. And they'll be so proud. (Did you think about the fact that if you don't graduate, you'll be keeping your parents from one of their proudest moments?) You've worked long and hard for that day, Evan. Don't throw it away.

body—the paragraphs that follow the salutation

But on the serious side, if you don't graduate you can probably give up your dream of owning your own computer graphics business. I don't know many colleges that would accept you without a high school diploma. And I think most computer businesses would be reluctant to hire you. So how will you get the training or the experience you need, not to mention a business loan? If you drop out, you could end up flipping burgers for a long time. And that would be a sad waste of your talents.

I know it's tempting, but dropping out of school just isn't worth it. We've only got a few more months 'til June. What do you say we stick it out together? I want you to be at my graduation party, Evan. But more importantly, I want to be at yours. Call me if you want to talk.

closing—a word or phrase that signals the end of the letter

Love,

signature—the writer's name

Jenny

BUSINESS LETTER

Depending on the prompt, you could be asked to do any of the four types of writing in a business letter.

Read the prompt to the right. Then notice the elements of an expository essay in the business letter that follows.

Prompt

In the Help Wanted section of your local newspaper, you spot the perfect part-time job. Write a letter to Miss Marlee Johnston, the company's personnel manager. Explain why you would be perfect for the job. Note: You can select any job that's right for you.

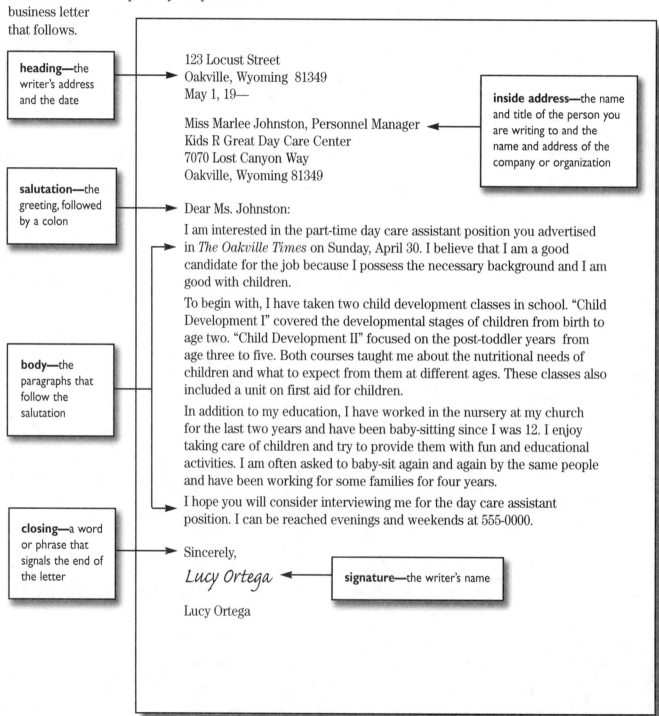

heading—the writer's address and the date

123 Locust Street
Oakville, Wyoming 81349
May 1, 19—

inside address—the name and title of the person you are writing to and the name and address of the company or organization

Miss Marlee Johnston, Personnel Manager
Kids R Great Day Care Center
7070 Lost Canyon Way
Oakville, Wyoming 81349

salutation—the greeting, followed by a colon

Dear Ms. Johnston:

I am interested in the part-time day care assistant position you advertised in *The Oakville Times* on Sunday, April 30. I believe that I am a good candidate for the job because I possess the necessary background and I am good with children.

To begin with, I have taken two child development classes in school. "Child Development I" covered the developmental stages of children from birth to age two. "Child Development II" focused on the post-toddler years from age three to five. Both courses taught me about the nutritional needs of children and what to expect from them at different ages. These classes also included a unit on first aid for children.

body—the paragraphs that follow the salutation

In addition to my education, I have worked in the nursery at my church for the last two years and have been baby-sitting since I was 12. I enjoy taking care of children and try to provide them with fun and educational activities. I am often asked to baby-sit again and again by the same people and have been working for some families for four years.

I hope you will consider interviewing me for the day care assistant position. I can be reached evenings and weekends at 555-0000.

closing—a word or phrase that signals the end of the letter

Sincerely,

Lucy Ortega

signature—the writer's name

Lucy Ortega

LETTER TO THE EDITOR

A letter to the editor prompt will require you to write a formal letter expressing your opinion on an issue. But, depending on the prompt, you could be asked to do any of the four types of writing.

Read the prompt above. Then notice the elements of both narrative and descriptive writing in the response that follows.

Prompt

You have recently read about a proposed plan to tear down your old elementary school and build a new one in its place. Write a letter to the editor that expresses your feelings on this plan. Include a story you remember from your years at the school to reinforce your opinion.

January 8, 19— ← **date**—the day, month, and year the letter is written

Dear Editor:

salutation— the greeting, followed by a colon

I recently read in your newspaper that the school board is proposing tearing down George Washington Carver Elementary and building a new one in its place. I believe it would be a shame to destroy such a wonderful old building.

I'll never forget my first day at Carver. Walking up to the building for the first time was awe-inspiring for a five-year-old. The double doors were so heavy it took both of my brother's hands and all his strength to open one. Wedging ourselves through the door, we entered the hallway, my new tennis shoes squeaking loudly against the shiny marble floors. As we started hand in hand down the hall, with my brother, I couldn't help being impressed (and a little bit intimidated) by the stateliness of the ornate ceilings, the gleaming white columns, and the bigger-than-life-sized murals of George Washington Carver on the walls. Even the metal lockers, lined up like soldiers against the wall, convinced me that I was there for a serious purpose. To me, the whole atmosphere of the building said "Education." How many of the new informal, ranch-style school buildings with dinosaur reading lofts and open-space classrooms can make the same claim today?

body— paragraphs that follow the salutation

It seems as if our only solution to aging buildings is to tear them down and replace them with new, inferior ones. Isn't there anything to be said for the quality of construction that originally went into that building? Even if remodeling costs as much as building a new one, isn't such a civic treasure worth it? George Washington Carver Elementary is a monument one of America's greatest scientists and to the quality of education that has always been provided there. Do we really want to risk losing all that?

closing—a word or phrase that signals the end of the letter

Sincerely,

Thomas J. Fuller

signature—the writer's name and address

Thomas J. Fuller
201 Northwest Oak Street
Bluff City, MO 55555

REPORT

Some writing tests may require you to compose a report based on a situation and notes provided in the prompt. Since a report is informational, it normally involves expository writing.

Read the prompt and the notes below. Then notice the elements of expository writing in report on the next page.

Prompt

Your history class has been learning about the westward expansion of the United States. For your class project, you have decided to write a report about Custer's Last Stand. You have done some research by reading several historical accounts of the famous battle. The notes you took while reading about this topic are listed below. Organize the notes into a written report. Be sure to

- Keep in mind that you are writing the report for your history class.

- Rearrange the notes before you start to write.

- Include all the information from the notes in your report.

Notes

Benteen's group joined Reno in hills

Captain Benteen's group traveled south to prevent Sioux from escaping

Custer thought soldiers could easily defeat village

Early on June 25, 1876, scouts found Sioux village in Little Bighorn River valley

Custer thought 1,000 warriors were in village; really more than 2,000 from various Sioux tribes—led by Crazy Horse and Sitting Bull

Indians fought Reno and Benteen's groups until June 26; then Indians disbanded and left territory

George Armstrong Custer—commanded the Seventh Cavalry Regiment

Custer's group headed downstream to attack weak point in village

Custer divided regiment into three groups

Major Reno's group was to cross river and attack village

Reno's troops met with fierce opposition and retreated to hills on opposite side of river

Custer's assignment was to round up Sioux and Cheyenne Indians and take to reservations

Sioux killed Custer and entire unit of 210 soldiers

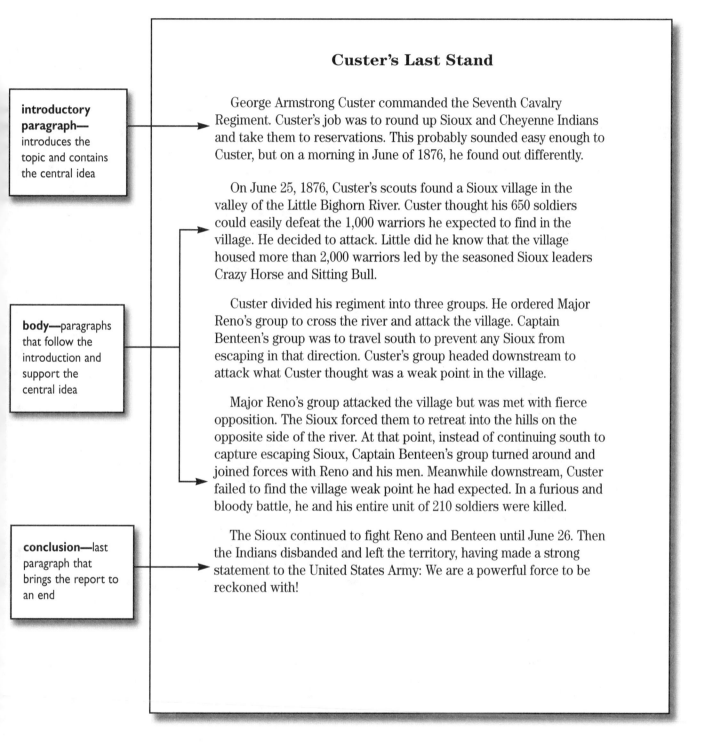

introductory paragraph— introduces the topic and contains the central idea

body— paragraphs that follow the introduction and support the central idea

conclusion— last paragraph that brings the report to an end

Custer's Last Stand

George Armstrong Custer commanded the Seventh Cavalry Regiment. Custer's job was to round up Sioux and Cheyenne Indians and take them to reservations. This probably sounded easy enough to Custer, but on a morning in June of 1876, he found out differently.

On June 25, 1876, Custer's scouts found a Sioux village in the valley of the Little Bighorn River. Custer thought his 650 soldiers could easily defeat the 1,000 warriors he expected to find in the village. He decided to attack. Little did he know that the village housed more than 2,000 warriors led by the seasoned Sioux leaders Crazy Horse and Sitting Bull.

Custer divided his regiment into three groups. He ordered Major Reno's group to cross the river and attack the village. Captain Benteen's group was to travel south to prevent any Sioux from escaping in that direction. Custer's group headed downstream to attack what Custer thought was a weak point in the village.

Major Reno's group attacked the village but was met with fierce opposition. The Sioux forced them to retreat into the hills on the opposite side of the river. At that point, instead of continuing south to capture escaping Sioux, Captain Benteen's group turned around and joined forces with Reno and his men. Meanwhile downstream, Custer failed to find the village weak point he had expected. In a furious and bloody battle, he and his entire unit of 210 soldiers were killed.

The Sioux continued to fight Reno and Benteen until June 26. Then the Indians disbanded and left the territory, having made a strong statement to the United States Army: We are a powerful force to be reckoned with!

On Your Own

Now it's your turn to respond to a prompt from one of the other types of writing tests. Choose one of the following prompts.

Prompt

Report

Your English class has been studying poets of the 20th century. For your class project, you have decided to write a report about Robert Frost. You have done some research by reading several biographies of the poet and a book of his collected poems. The notes you took while reading about Frost are listed to the right. Organize the notes into a written report. Be sure to

- Keep in mind that you are writing the report for your English class.
- Rearrange the notes before you start to write.
- Include all the information from the notes in your report.

Notes

Robert Lee Frost:

Born in San Francisco in 1874 but family moved to New England in 1885 after his father's death

Most popular poet of his time

Was known as a pastoral poet: one who wrote about rural themes

Won Pulitzer Prize for poetry four times

Received a gold medal from Congress in 1960 "in recognition of his poetry, which has enriched the culture of the United States and the philosophy of the world"

Read his poem "The Gift Outright" at Pres. Kennedy's inauguration in 1961

Worked in New England as farmer, editor, and school teacher

Found inspiration for his poetry in the New England area

Poetry is noted for its plain language, traditional form, and graceful style

Believed nature's secrets could never be known

Humanity's best chance for happiness involved working usefully and productively: significant toil

Frost succeeded in realizing his life's ambition: to write "a few poems it will be hard to get rid of"

Died 1963

Prompt

Letter to the Editor

Your city is considering discontinuing its curbside recycling program because the program is very costly. Write a letter to the editor that expresses your opinion of the idea

Prompt

Business Letter

Your city council is considering passing a curfew law for teenagers. Write a letter to the council that expresses your point of view on the idea of curfews.

Prompt

Friendly Letter

Write a letter to a relative telling him or her about your plans for the next several years of your life.

COMMON PROBLEM AREAS IN ESSAY WRITING

Everyone makes mistakes in writing, especially when working within a time limit. What follows are some common problem areas in essays written by high school students. Read through each problem area. Then complete the exercises that accompany each. Learning how to avoid these problems now can result in a better essay—and a better test score.

PRONOUN REFERENCE

A pronoun is a word that takes the place of a noun or another pronoun. An antecedent is the word that the pronoun replaces. Read the examples below.

> **As You Write...**
> Note each pronoun. Make sure it makes a clear, correct reference to its antecedent.

        ant.   pro.

EXAMPLE   *Gabe took **his** dog for a walk.*

In the above sentence, "Gabe" is the antecedent, and "his" is the pronoun that takes its place.

        ant.   pro.   pro.   pro.

EXAMPLE   ***Shannon** takes **her** laptop computer with **her** everywhere **she** goes.*

In this sentence, "Shannon" is the antecedent, and "her," "her," and "she" are the pronouns that take its place. Pronouns help writers avoid awkward sentences like, "Shannon takes Shannon's laptop computer with Shannon everywhere Shannon goes."

The most common pronoun reference problems fall under two categories: incorrect number reference and ambiguous (unclear) reference.

Incorrect Number Reference

Incorrect number reference occurs when the pronoun and antecedent don't match in number. Look at the examples and revisions below.

EXAMPLE   *Each student should bring **their** lunch.*

The antecedent "each student" is singular; therefore, the pronoun that replaces it must be singular.

REVISION   *Each student should bring **his** or **her** lunch. OR All students should bring **their** lunches.*

continued

EXAMPLE   *Did **either** of the girls actually believe **they** would get away with cheating?*

The antecedent "either" is singular; therefore, the pronoun must also be singular.

REVISION   *Did **either** of the girls believe **she** would get away with cheating?*

Such words as "each," "few," and "any" are called indefinite pronouns. Some indefinite pronouns are always singular, and some are always plural. Others are singular or plural, depending on their antecedents.

Here is a table of indefinite pronouns.

Indefinite Pronouns

Always Singular	Always Plural	Singular or Plural
anybody	both	all
anyone	few	any
each	many	most
either	several	more
everybody		some
everyone		
neither		
none		
one		
somebody		
someone		

Directions: Circle the correct pronouns and nouns from the parentheses in each item. Refer to the table above if necessary.

1. Everyone must take (his or her, their) turn.

2. Neither of the bicycles is worth (its, their) price.

3. Each of the girls does (her, their) own cooking.

4. Several of the boys built (his, their) own (go cart, go carts) for the fair.

5. No one could find (his or her, their) way in the storm.

As You Write...
If you don't know whether an indefinite pronoun such as "all" or "some" is singular or plural, try using it with different verbs. Decide which sounds right and go with it.

Ambiguous Reference

Ambiguous reference occurs when it is unclear which antecedent a pronoun is replacing. Look at the examples and revisions below.

EXAMPLE   *The men removed all the furniture from the room to clean it.*

It is unclear in the above sentence whether "it" refers to the room or the furniture.

REVISION   *The men removed all the furniture from the room and then cleaned the room. OR After removing all the furniture, the men cleaned the room.*

EXAMPLE   *Luis should help John, but he should help himself first.*

Should Luis help himself or should John help himself?

REVISION   *Luis should help John, but Luis should help himself first. OR Luis should help himself before he helps John.*

EXAMPLE   *Sylvia told Emma that she had made a mistake.*

Who made the mistake, Sylvia or Emma?

REVISION   *Sylvia said to Emma, "I made a mistake." OR Sylvia admitted that she had made a mistake to Emma.*

Directions: The following sentences contain ambiguous pronoun references. Write a corrected version of each.

1. Hunters should be careful how they carry their guns when they are loaded.

2. The President appointed Senator Hudson as chairman because he was concerned with the environment.

3. We unpacked our dishes from the moving boxes and then sold them to the family next door.

4. Connie did a wonderful chalk drawing of her cat and then hung it on her wall.

5. After the student helpers cleared the table, the janitor wiped them down.

SENTENCE ERRORS

Two kinds of sentence errors are common in high school essays: sentence fragments and sentence run-ons. A *sentence fragment* is an incomplete sentence punctuated as a complete sentence. A *run-on sentence* occurs when two or more sentences are written as though they were one sentence.

While you might often speak in fragments and sometimes even in run-ons, the formal nature of an essay requires you to use properly structured sentences. Complete, well-structured sentences will work best to express your ideas.

Sentence Fragments

In order for a group of words to be a complete sentence, it must

- Have a subject, either stated or implied.
- Have a verb.
- Express a complete thought.

> ### As You Write...
> Check your sentences carefully to see where one thought ends and the next begins. Remember that the punctuation you've included should match the thoughts you've expressed.

A group of words is a sentence fragment if it is lacking any of the above elements. Sentence fragments can be revised by making them into complete sentences or by incorporating them into existing sentences. Sentence fragments normally fall into two categories: phrase fragments and subordinate clause fragments.

Phrase Fragments

A *phrase* is a group of words that does not contain a subject and a verb. A phrase fragment is usually part of a nearby sentence. Read the examples of phrase fragments in italics below. Then read the revisions.

EXAMPLE This morning I saw Julio. *Jogging in the park.*

The phrase "jogging in the park" modifies the noun "Julio." It should be included in the sentence with the word it modifies.

REVISION *This morning I saw Julio jogging in the park.*

EXAMPLE The children played at the north end of the playground. *Under the stand of oak trees.*

The phrase "Under the stand of oak trees" modifies the verb "played" and should be included in the sentence with the word it modifies.

REVISION *The children played at the north end of the playground under the stand of oak trees.*

EXAMPLE   To work with animals. *That's what I want to do when I grow up.*

The phrase "to work with animals" should be placed in the sentence with the idea it explains, "what I want to do when I grow up."

REVISION   *What I want to do when I grow up is work with animals.*

EXAMPLE   Jill's mother came home from her business trip bearing gifts. *A CD for her daughter and a watch for her husband.*

The phrase "A CD for her daughter and a watch for her husband" refers back to "gifts" and should be joined to that word with a comma.

REVISION   *Jill's mother came home from her business trip bearing gifts, a CD for her daughter and a watch for her husband.*

Subordinate Clause Fragments

A *clause* is a group of words that contains a subject and a verb. A clause can be either independent or subordinate (dependent). An *independent clause* (also known as a simple sentence) expresses a complete thought and is therefore a sentence. Below is an example of an independent clause.

EXAMPLE   *The Fairview Giants won the championship.*

A *subordinate clause* depends upon an independent clause for meaning and, therefore, can never be written as a sentence in itself. Notice the independent clause and the subordinate clause in the example below.

<table>
<tr><td>subordinate clause</td><td>independent clause</td></tr>
</table>

EXAMPLE   *Even though odds were against them, the Fairview Giants won the championship.*

<table>
<tr><td>subject verb</td><td>subject   verb</td></tr>
</table>

"Even though odds were against them" is not a complete thought. In order to make sense, it must be combined with the independent clause "the Fairview Giants won the championship." Otherwise the reader will find himself asking, "Even though the odds were against them' what?"

Here is another example of a sentence that contains both an independent and a subordinate clause.

<table>
<tr><td>independent clause</td><td>subordinate clause</td></tr>
</table>

EXAMPLE   *Kelly could be a good pitcher if he would practice more.*

<table>
<tr><td>subject verb</td><td>subject   verb</td></tr>
</table>

Again, the subordinate clause "if he would practice more" depends upon the independent clause "Kelly could be a good pitcher" to make sense.

continued

Subordinate clauses start with subordinating conjunctions. Below is a list of the most common subordinating conjunctions. Becoming familiar with them now can help you avoid sentence fragments in your writing.

Common Subordinating Conjunctions

after	even though	unless
although	if	until
as	in order that	when
as if	since	whenever
as long as	so that	where
because	than	wherever
before	though	while

Run-On Sentences

A *run-on sentence* is two or more independent clauses that are treated as one sentence. There are two types of run-on sentences. The first consists of two sentences that are run together without punctuation between them. The other occurs when two sentences are separated by a comma instead of a period. See the example of the first type below.

EXAMPLE   *Buying a stereo is difficult there are so many models on the market.*

There are several ways to revise the above example.

Separate with a period

REVISION   *Buying a stereo is difficult. There are so many models on the market.*

Separate with a semicolon

REVISION   *Buying a stereo is difficult; there are so many models on the market.*

Join with a subordinating conjunction (because)

REVISION   *Buying a stereo is difficult because there are so many models on the market.*

The other type of run-on sentence, also known as a comma splice, is shown below.

EXAMPLE   *The team lost six games, at least three losses were due to fumbles.*

Again, there is more than one way to fix this type of run-on.

Separate with a period

REVISION   *The team lost six games. At least three losses were due to fumbles.*

Separate with a semicolon

REVISION   *The team lost six games; at least three losses were due to fumbles.*

Leave the comma and join the two sentences with a coordinating conjunction (and)

REVISION   *The team lost six games, and at least three losses were due to fumbles.*

Directions: The following is the first body paragraph of an essay written in response to a prompt concerning the issue of installing video games in a school cafeteria to raise money. The paragraph contains several sentence fragments and run-on sentences. Rewrite the paragraph, using the methods described in this section.

If video games were installed in the cafeteria, students might spend their lunch money on the games. Instead of on lunch. Parents send their children to school. Assuming that they will receive a nutritious meal at lunchtime. If students skip lunch in order to play video games, their performance in afternoon classes could suffer their grades may drop and they may become ineligible for extracurricular activities. Bad grades could even keep them out of college, in short, students' futures could suffer. To prevent kids from being tempted to spend their money on video games instead of lunch, the games should not be placed in the cafeteria.

SUBJECT/VERB AGREEMENT

A subject and a verb "agree" if both are singular or both are plural. In the following examples, the subjects and verbs agree.

sing. subject   sing. verb

EXAMPLE   *Kelvin skillfully **handles** a basketball.*

The singular subject "Kelvin" agrees with the singular verb "handles."

plural subject   plural verb

EXAMPLE   *Kelvin and James skillfully **handle** a basketball.*

The plural, or compound, subject "Kelvin and James" agrees with the plural verb "handle."

By this time, you probably have little trouble with subject/verb agreement when the subject of a sentence directly precedes the verb. However, many agreement problems occur when the subject and verb are interrupted by a phrase.

Phrase Interrupters

The subject of a sentence can be hard to locate if a phrase comes between the subject and its verb. Look at the following example. Notice how the insertion of a phrase can cause confusion in locating the subject of the sentence.

subject

EXAMPLE   *This **batch** is ready to be sold.*

subject   phrase interrupter

EXAMPLE   *This **batch of cute, little kittens** is ready to be sold.*

"Batch" is still the subject of the second sentence; therefore, its verb is still the singular verb "is." Keep in mind that an interrupting phrase, such as "of cute, little kittens," does not change the subject in number.

> **As You Write...**
> Compare your subjects to their verbs. Make sure both are either singular or plural. Don't confuse a phrase interrupter with the subject of your sentence.

ACTIVITY   **Directions:** Underline the subject of each of the following sentences. Then circle the correct form of the verb from the choices in parentheses.

1. The Lions is one of those teams that (rally, rallies) late in the game.

2. The coach, as well as the fans, (was were) disappointed in the team's performance.

3. The arrival of the new costumes (has, have) caused excitement among the cast of the play.

4. The artwork, in addition to the jewelry, (are, is) to be auctioned off in May.

5. An acre of trees and meadows (surround, surrounds) the house.

POINT OF VIEW

Point of view in essay writing refers to the perspective from which the writer communicates with the reader. The point of view you use depends on the type of writing you are doing. The important thing to remember is to avoid shifting from one point of view to another.

As You Write...
Look for shifts in point of view. Maintaining a third-person point of view means eliminating pronous like "I," "you," and "we" and replacing them with neutral terms such as "one," "a person," or "most people."

first-person point of view—In first-person point of view, the narrator discusses the subject of the essay "from within" the story. He or she may be a character in the story or a witness to the event. The narrator will use "I" and "we" freely. The following example demonstrates the first-person point of view.

> I knew when I woke up this morning that this was going to be a bad day. First of all, we lost our electricity during the night because of a thunderstorm, so my alarm didn't go off. I woke up at 7:15, and I had to catch the bus at 7:30—no time for a shower or for breakfast. Then I got to school and found that the locker I share with my best friend had been vandalized. We both had our gym shoes stolen, and our books and papers were covered with shaving cream and chocolate syrup.

third-person point of view—The narrator discusses the subject "from without." He or she is removed from any participation in the subject matter. In third-person, the narrator usually does not use "I" or "we." The following paragraph demonstrates the third-person point of view.

> When Phillip awoke that morning, it didn't take him long to figure out that it was going to be a bad day. First of all, his alarm didn't go off because a storm had caused the electricity to go out during the night. He didn't wake up until 7:15 and had to be on the bus by 7:30. He had no time to take a shower or eat breakfast. Then when he got to school, he found that the locker he shared with his best friend had been vandalized. Both boys had their gym shoes stolen, and their books and papers were covered with shaving cream and chocolate syrup.

Expository and Persuasive Writing

The formal nature of third-person point of view makes it ideal for expository, or informational, essays. And persuasive essays that cover a general issue, such as whether music lyrics should be subject to censorship, are also written from the third-person perspective. However, if you are writing about a personal issue, such as whether students at your school should be allowed to leave the campus for lunch, you may choose to use first-person point of view.

continued

Narrative and Descriptive Writing

Many narrative and descriptive writing prompts focus on personal experiences or emotions. For example, you might be asked to relate the story of a mistake you made in your life, or you might be expected to describe how a particular type of music makes you feel. Some narrative prompts ask you to create a fictional story, and some descriptive prompts ask you to describe a location, such as the school cafeteria at lunchtime.

Because of the varying nature of narrative and descriptive writing, no one point of view is recommended. If the prompt focuses on a personal experience or emotion, you will probably want to use first-person. Otherwise use third. Again, the important thing to remember is to avoid shifting from one point of view to another.

Directions: The following paragraph is supposed to be written from a third-person point of view. Circle the numbers of the sentences that contain a point of view shift. Then rewrite each of the sentences so it reflects the third-person point of view.

(1) Technology is a scary word to many people. (2) Some feel that it's because technology involves machinery and that people have a basic distrust of machinery. (3) I think this is probably true. (4) After all, how many horror stories have we all read about machines that somehow come to life and turn against people? (5) On a more realistic scale, how many people have experienced a malfunction in a computer system that resulted in inaccurate records? (6) Sometimes these "glitches" take months to clear up. (7) Today everything in our society seems to be run by some kind of computer. (8) And the computers that scientists are building are "smarter" than ever! (9) When you stop to think that the advancement of technology led to the development of the nuclear bomb, it's no wonder people are uneasy. (10) These people deserve our empathy.

EFFECTIVE DETAILS

When you describe something with words, you want your readers to form the same picture in their minds as you have in yours. Below are three ways you can use details to bring your writing to life.

Show, Don't Tell

Avoid telling your readers what to see, hear, touch, smell, or taste. Instead, show them by providing a good, clear description of your experience. If you provide a clear description, readers will naturally share your experience.

Compare the following sentences. Mark the one that provides the reader with a clearer picture.

❏ *The heat in the car made me uncomfortable. Every time I moved it got worse. I was really miserable.*

❏ *Every time I moved, the vinyl seat cover tugged at the skin on my legs. Drops of perspiration trickled down my back. The sweat gathered at my waistband, creating a belt of dampness around my waist.*

Use Vivid Words

Develop the habit of using vivid, specific words in your writing in place of vague or general words. Vivid words help readers visualize your subject.

Compare the following pairs of sentences. Mark the one that provides the reader with a clearer picture.

❏ *The eagle flew above the canyon, searching for food.*

❏ *The eagle soared above the canyon, searching for an unwary mouse or a careless rabbit.*

Provide Examples

Complete your descriptions by providing examples. Examples further explain your topic for the readers, providing them with the clearest possible picture.

Compare the following sentences. Mark the one that gives the reader a clearer picture.

❏ *Sasha is a dependable friend. She does anything for me.*

❏ *Sasha is a dependable friend. When my car wouldn't start, she dropped everything, drove to my house, and took me to work.*

continued

Clichés

If you think you have heard a description a hundred times, more than likely it is a cliché. Clichés are phrases like "scared to death" and "worth its weight in gold" that are so overused that they are no longer effective.

Compare the following details. Mark the one that provides the reader with a clearer picture.

❑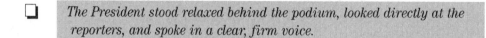
The President was as cool as a cucumber at the press conference.

❑
The President stood relaxed behind the podium, looked directly at the reporters, and spoke in a clear, firm voice.

 **Directions:** Rewrite the following details, using the method indicated in parentheses.

1. Nelson walked out the door, obviously pleased with himself. (Use vivid words.)

2. Rip is an old dog. (Show, don't tell.)

3. The scream from the attic scared me to death. (Avoid clichés.)

4. My cousin is such a brat. (Provide examples.)

5. Alan read the book quickly while eating a hurried breakfast. (Use vivid words.)

As You Write...

Check to see that your details are clear and that there are enough of them. Make sure your details provide readers with the same "picture" you have in your mind.

ACTIVE AND PASSIVE VOICE

One of the easiest and most effective skills you can develop in your writing is to use the active voice whenever possible. In *active voice*, the subject of the sentence is the actor; in other words, the subject performs the action. Here is an example of a sentence written in active voice.

EXAMPLE

    actor   action   acted-upon

Antonio kicked the ball.

    subject

In *passive voice*, the subject of the sentence is acted upon by someone or something. Read the example below.

EXAMPLE

    acted-upon   action   actor

The ball was kicked by Antonio.

    subject

As the examples show, active voice provides the reader with a clearer picture than passive voice. In active voice the reader can actually see Antonio kicking the ball. The action in the passive voice example, "was kicked," is vague. Also, passive voice requires more words than active voice. In the examples above, the active voice sentence contains four words; the passive voice sentence contains six.

Besides providing clarity, active voice enables you to write concisely, something every writer should strive for.

When to Use Passive Voice

While active voice is generally recommended in writing, passive voice can be effective if used properly. The following examples show effective uses of passive voice.

Use passive voice when the actor is less important than what is acted upon.

EXAMPLE

    acted-upon   action   actor

Blizzard warnings were issued by the ***National Weather Service*** *well in advance of the storm.* (The fact that the blizzard warnings were issued is more important than who issued them.)

Use passive voice when the actor is unknown.

EXAMPLE

    acted-upon   action

The ***downtown branch*** *of the First National Bank* ***was robbed*** *last night.* (It is not known who robbed the bank.)

continued

Changing Passive Voice to Active Voice

Three methods for "activating" passive voice are listed below.

1. *Reverse the order of the actor and the acted-upon.*

	acted-upon	action	actor
PASSIVE	*The car wash was sponsored by the art club.*		

	actor		acted-upon
ACTIVE	*The art club sponsored the car wash.*		

2. *Change the verb.*

		verb	
ACTIVE	*Sharone **was given** a CD player for her birthday.*		

		verb	
PASSIVE	*Sharone **received** a CD player for her birthday.*		

3. *If the actor is not mentioned, supply one.*

ACTIVE	*The ball was hit to center field.* (Who hit the ball?)

	actor
PASSIVE	*Jackie hit the ball to center field.*

> **As You Write...**
> Look for overuse of the passive voice. Activate whenever necessary.

Directions: As you copy the following sentences, activate the passive verbs using one of the methods listed above. Try to use each method at least once. Write the number of the method you used beside your answer. If you think passive voice is acceptable, write "acceptable" and explain why.

1. An exciting game was expected that night.

2. The land for the new library was purchased by the city last February.

3. Oddly enough, the door was unlocked when we arrived.

4. The new strategy was completely forgotten by the team.

5. Smoking is not allowed in our building.

PARALLEL STRUCTURE

Parallel structure is the repetition of a grammatical structure. Parallel structures, or parallelisms, are often used for ideas that are similar or are of equal importance. Parallelisms aid your readers' understanding because readers are able to relate one idea to another.

Read the examples of faulty parallel structure below. Then read the corrected versions that follow each.

FAULTY
> *The teacher told the students **to read** the chapter, **to take notes** on it, and **that they should prepare for a test** on the material.*

CORRECT
> *The teacher told the students **to read** the chapter, **to take notes** on it, and **to prepare** for a test on the material.*

An *infinitive* consists of a verb plus the preposition "to." "To read" and "to take" are infinitives; therefore, in order for the series in the first sentence to be parallel, "that they should prepare" should be rewritten as "to prepare."

FAULTY
> *In my report, I will discuss **the origin of rock and roll** music and **how it has progressed.***

CORRECT
> *In my report, I will discuss the **origin** and **progress** of rock and roll music.*

In the first sentence, "origin" is a noun; therefore, in order for the sentence to be parallel, "how it has progressed" should be changed to the noun "progress." (Alternatively, the sentence could be rewritten as "In my report, I will discuss how rock and roll music **originated** and how it *has progressed.)*

FAULTY
> *Carol is **attractive, intelligent,** and **has a quick wit.***

CORRECT
> *Carol is **attractive, intelligent,** and **quick-witted.***

"Attractive" and "intelligent" are adjectives; therefore, "has a quick wit" should be changed to the adjective "quick-witted."

As You Write...
Check to see that words or phrases in a series are parallel.

continued

Directions: Correct the faulty parallel structure in the following sentences.

1. Ho's speech was inaccurate and annoyed a lot of people.

2. The desk had a scratched top, a sticky drawer, and one leg wobbled.

3. To me, summer is the smell of mowed grass, the sound of outdoor concerts, and the way hamburgers taste on the grill.

4. The danger with gases is that many are invisible and can't be tasted.

5. The people of Mexico and the Canadians are our closest neighbors.

Parallel Structure for Effect

Parallelisms give your writing a rhythm, thus making your writing flow. Also, through the use of repetition, parallelisms emphasize your ideas and add style to your writing. Read the examples of effective parallelisms below.

EXAMPLE *Ask not what your country can do for you; ask what you can do for your country.*—John F. Kennedy

EXAMPLE *It was the best of times, it was the worst of times.*—Charles Dickens

EXAMPLE *When people tell you how young you look, they are also telling you how old you are.* —Cary Grant

Now read the same examples written without attention to parallel structure.

EXAMPLE *Ask not what your country can do for you; find out how you can help your country.*

EXAMPLE *It was the best of times, also the times were bad.*

EXAMPLE *When people tell you how young you look, they are also saying you are old.*

Directions: The following quotations were originally parallel in structure. Revise the italicized section of each sentence so that it is parallel with the first part of the sentence.

EXAMPLE

Contentment consists not in great wealth, but *in not wanting very many things.*
—Epictetus

REVISION

Contentment consists not in great wealth, but in few wants.

1. A single death is a tragedy, *it's a statistic when a million people die.*—Joseph Stalin

2. If the very old will remember, *listening will occur among the very young.*
   —Chief Dan George

3. We must learn to live together as brothers or *we will become fools and perish as a group.*
   —Martin Luther King, Jr.

4. It's not the men in my life that count—*it's how lively they are.*—Mae West

5. Becoming number one is easier than *to be able to stay in first place.*—Bill Bradley

6. Everyone thinks of changing the world, but *a person doesn't think about the fact that he might change.*—Leo Tolstoy

7. In the factory we make cosmetics; *hope is sold in the drugstore.*—Charles Revson

8. Mankind must put an end to war, *or we will all be killed by war.*—John F. Kennedy

9. One man's terrorist is *a freedom fighter to other men.*—Yonan Alexander

10. In peace, sons bury their fathers; *during a time of war, sons are buried by their fathers.*
    —Herodotus

SENTENCE VARIETY

Variety is the key to interesting, readable sentences. As you read the paragraph to the right, notice how every sentence "sounds" the same.

Original Paragraph

It was Emma's birthday. Kevin had no ideas for a gift. He wandered the mall. He talked to some clerks. He came away empty-handed. Then he looked through catalogs. He was disappointed at what he saw. Her birthday was only a few days away. Kevin was beginning to panic.

The sentences below demonstrate how a little knowledge of grammar and sentence structure can make it easy for you to transform a simple and humdrum pattern of words into a sentence with "life." (The groups of words in italics are grammatically defined in parentheses. Refer to the glossary at the back of this book if you are unfamiliar with any of the terms.)

1. *It was Emma's birthday. Kevin had no ideas for a gift.* (two simple sentences)

2. *Kevin had no ideas, and Emma had no birthday gift.* (two independent clauses joined by a comma and the coordinating conjunction "and")

3. *Kevin had no ideas; Emma had no birthday gift.* (two independent clauses joined by a semicolon)

4. *Buying the right birthday gift for Emma* required a good idea from Kevin. (gerund phrase)

5. *Because he lacked ideas,* Kevin had not bought Emma a birthday gift. (introductory subordinate clause)

6. *What could Kevin buy Emma for her birthday?* He had no idea. (interrogative)

7. *Without an idea in mind,* Kevin had not bought Emma's birthday gift. (introductory prepositional phrase)

8. Kevin, *Emma's boyfriend,* had no idea what to buy Emma for her birthday. (appositive which defines the noun "Kevin")

9. *In order to buy Emma the perfect gift,* Kevin needed one thing: *an idea.* (introductory prepositional phrase; appositive which further defines the noun "thing")

10. Kevin, *who was suffering from a lack of ideas,* had bought nothing for Emma's birthday. (relative clause which modifies the noun "Kevin")

Read the revised version of the paragraph below. Numbers of the sentence patterns are given in parentheses.

Revised Paragraph

Kevin, Emma's boyfriend, had no idea what to buy Emma for her birthday. (8) He wandered the mall and talked to some clerks, but he came away empty-handed. (2) Looking through catalogs only made Kevin disappointed. (4) Because her birthday was only a few days away, Kevin was beginning to panic. (5)

Directions: Now choose two of the following pairs of sentences and transform them into five sentences with variety. Pattern your sentences after the ones in the chart on the previous page or combine the patterns to create your own structures. Add additional words or details as necessary. A suggestion for the first one has been provided.

1. Abdul shook his head and sighed. The experiment was a failure.

   EXAMPLE The experiment, which was a failure, caused Abdul to shake his head and sigh. (pattern #10)

2. The baby cried for her pacifier. The young father stumbled out of bed in response.

3. Carmen looked forward to Saturday night. She hoped to see Bernardo at the dance.

4. The hikers took the wrong trail. They wandered aimlessly for hours.

5. Paige tried to study for the SAT exam. She couldn't concentrate with her brother's stereo blaring in the next room.

As You Write...
Check your sentence for length and structure. Vary your sentences by adding phrases or clauses. Try combining short, choppy sentences for a smoother effect and breaking up sentences that are too long.

Directions: The following paragraph is made up entirely of simple sentences. Transform it into a paragraph with "life" by rewriting it, using several of the patterns presented earlier.

Galileo turned his primitive telescope on the planet Saturn. He did this in the year 1610. He was surprised. The planet seemed to have two large ears! Christiaan Huygens studied Saturn. He did this in 1655. He determined that the "ears" were really rings. Both scientists would be surprised at what astonomers know today. They know that at least two other planets have rings.

_____

_____

_____

_____

TRANSITIONS

When you're speaking to someone, you can easily convey a shift in meaning by using gestures or changing your facial expression or tone of voice. However, when you write, your readers can't hear your voice inflections or see your body language. To convey such cues, use transitions in your writing. Transitions guide the reader smoothly from one idea to the next. There are two main types of transitions in essay writing: transitions within paragraphs and transitions between paragraphs.

Transitions Within Paragraphs

The transitions within your paragraphs indicate how your details are linked. Below are some commonly used transitions you can use in your writing.

To introduce an example	To introduce or add to an idea	To indicate a contrasting idea	To indicate a conclusion or result
a case in point	after	conversely	accordingly
for example	also	despite this fact	as a result
to illustrate	equally important	however	clearly then
	finally	instead	consequently
	furthermore	nevertheless	finally
	in addition	on the contrary	in conclusion
	in the first, second place	on the other hand	in other words
	most importantly	still	in summary
	next		therefore
	to begin with		

Read through the paragraph on the right. Choose transitions from the above table to fill in the appropriate blanks.

    The most disastrous vacation I ever spent with my family was the year we went to Lake White Rock. _____, we had been told that our cabin overlooked the water. _____, while we could see the water, it was a 20-minute walk over hot concrete and burning sand. No problem had we had a car. _____, the family car broke down the second day we were there and spent the next three days in the local garage. _____, we had to walk or take a taxi wherever we went. _____, the weather was near 100 degrees the entire time, and the humidity was 95 percent, which is the reason we rented an air-conditioned cabin. _____, the air conditioning consisted of one overworked and undersized window unit that caught fire one day while we were gone. Luckily, it was a small fire. _____, we came back to find our belongings and our clothes smelling of smoke. We were moved to another cabin—even farther from the lake, of course. _____, we were determined to make the best of it. And we might have, had my dad not broken his leg water-skiing.
    _____, our vacation was cut short. We headed home with Dad in a cast, Mom driving, and the rest of us in very bad moods.

Transitions Between Paragraphs

The beginning of a new body paragraph signals the reader that you're moving on to the next phase of your paper. Make this shift clear by providing an appropriate transition. Such a transition should show the relationship between the current and the next paragraphs. One of the best ways to achieve this transition is to insert a significant word, phrase, or idea from the first paragraph into the topic sentence of the second paragraph.

Following are the central idea and the first two body paragraphs of an essay written by Sarah in response to the prompt below. Notice how the topic sentence of the second body paragraph refers back to a significant idea from the first body paragraph.

> **As You Write...**
> Look for places where transitions should naturally occur. Use a caret (^) to insert a missing transition. Be sure to include transitional statements between main sections of your essay.

Prompt

Students often complain about their school lunch program. Think about ways lunch at your school could be made better. Now explain three ways to improve your lunch program.

Sarah's central idea: The lunch program at the high school could be improved by implementing an open campus policy, serving larger portions, and providing a wider variety of foods from which to choose.

The first way to improve lunch at the high school would be to allow students to leave the campus for lunch. Since most students would probably leave if allowed, open campus would result in the need for fewer lunch periods. Fewer lunch periods, in turn, could result in a shortened school day. Also, since fewer students would be eating school lunch, the cooks would have less food to prepare, which might possibly result in better food. Allowing students to leave the building for lunch would certainly be a step in the right direction to improving the high school's lunch program.

If an open campus policy is out of the question, the lunch program at the high school could be made more enjoyable if larger portions of food were served. One taco, a helping of corn, and a cookie is not enough to satisfy the stomachs of growing teenagers. As a result, students often end up buying second lunches. This, of course, is hard on the wallets of many students and/or parents. Larger portions would also leave students feeling more satisfied and energetic for their afternoon classes. Also, many students have extracurricular activities after school, and larger portions would help sustain them until they get home for dinner. Clearly, larger portions would make the lunch program a more enjoyable and satisfying experience for all.

continued

 **Directions:** Below is the first body paragraph of a student essay written in response to the following prompt. Create a topic sentence for the second body paragraph of the essay. Make sure the topic sentence you create contains an important idea from the first body paragraph.

Prompt

People usually become parents without any training. Some people are naturally good parents while others have to work at it. Based on your own experience as a son or daughter, think of three rules parents should follow to be good parents. Write a paper that explains the three most important rules of parenting from a son or daughter's perspective.

Natalie's central idea: Three specific rules come to mind when I think of "laying down the law" for my parents: Respect your children, listen to them before assuming things, and don't invade their privacy.

Body Paragraph #1

   The first rule of successful parenting is to respect your children. Parents sometimes assume that since they make the rules, they can treat children as less than people. Human beings deserve the same amount of respect, no matter what their age. For example, a child is not allowed to swear at a parent; the same rule should apply to parents directing profanity at children. Children are not expected to physically harm their parents. Parents, in turn, should not be allowed to hit their children. Children are supposed to abide by their parents' decisions. Parents should be the ones to make major decisions, but they should also ask for and consider their children's feelings before making those decisions. Anyone's parenting skills could be improved by simply respecting the younger people in the household.

Body Paragraph #2

topic sentence: _____

_____

_____

_____

WORDY WRITING

Many essay tests have length requirements. As a result, students often add fluff, or extra words, to their writing to "make the grade." But while fluff might add length to your essay, chances are it won't improve it. Good writing is clear and concise. It says exactly what needs to be said and uses only those words necessary to say it. Adding extra words for the sake of length will only clutter up your writing and make it harder for your readers to get your point.

> ### As You Write...
> Avoid inserting unnecessary words. Write as clearly and concisely as possible.

Read the examples of wordy writing below and the revised versions that follow.

EXAMPLE *It was two hours later that the people who were going to help us arrived.* (15 words)

REVISION *Two hours later help arrived.* **(5 words)**

EXAMPLE *The quarterback gained a distance of ten yards as he advanced forward down the field with the ball.* (18 words)

REVISION *The quarterback gained ten yards as he advanced with the ball.* (11 words)

Notice that the revised versions cut down on the wordiness of the examples without losing meaning. Remember that saying too much is as bad as saying too little. If you are trying to meet a length requirement, expand on your ideas, not on the quantity of your words.

ACTIVITY

Directions: The sentences below are too wordy. Rewrite each, eliminating the unnecessary words while retaining the meaning.

1. At this point in time, the consensus of opinion is that the actual facts in the case are few in number.

2. It was while practicing playing the piano that Sylvia heard a really strange noise.

3. There were several old desks lined up against the wall in the room.

4. The first thing that happened was that the burglar alarm failed to go off.

5. In addition, the Hawks' past record has also shown them to be equally as good as the Tigers at winning football games.

TEN TIPS FOR QUICK REVISION

More than likely, you won't have a lot of time to revise your writing in a test situation. That's why it's important to be able to decide quickly what to fix. As you read through your finished product, focus on the following elements and be ready to revise if necessary.

❑ Reread your central idea carefully. Make sure it indicates the exact contents of your paper.

❑ Check your body paragraphs for clarity. Clarify a sketchy detail by adding an additional line of elaboration in the margin.

❑ Look for words you might have omitted. Use a caret (^) to indicate where a word should be inserted; then write the word above the caret.

❑ Listen for natural pauses. Insert commas where necessary.

❑ Scan for capitalization. Make sure all words at the beginning of sentences, as well as any proper nouns, are capitalized. Cross through the word and write the capitalized version above.

❑ Look for misspelled words. If you find any, neatly draw a line through the word and rewrite the correctly spelled word above the misspelled one.

❑ Check to see that your sentences end in the appropriate end punctuation (period, question mark, or exclamation point).

❑ Make sure you have included transitions where needed. Again, use a caret (^) to indicate where a transition should be inserted. Then write the transition above the caret or in the margin.

❑ Look for words you might have written twice. Make a neat line through one of them.

❑ Listen for awkward wording. Remedy by neatly crossing through the word or phrase. Then place your revision above or in the margin.

Below is the introductory paragraph of a persuasive essay. Notice how the writer revised his writing using the tips listed on the preceding page.

○ Picture bees descending on a small flower patch. They push and

nectar
shove, scrambling to get their fill of ~~nectar~~ before it is time to

the
^
return to their hive. That is pretty much the scene in cafeteria every

With   fighting
day at lunchtime. ~~While~~ 350 students ~~fight~~ to get through four

○ lunch lines in 20 minutes, it is no wonder things get a little chaotic.

Unless
~~unless~~ you brown-bag it, you don't stand ~~much~~ much of a chance

at getting your food and actually being able to do anything but inhale

Without a doubt, the   ten
it. ^ ~~The~~ lunch shifts need to be extended by at least ~~10~~ minutes.

○

TEST-TAKING TIPS

Each chapter in this book offers tips and strategies that will help you in a writing test situation. Here are some additional tips.

1. Begin a writing test by quickly scanning all the prompts. This will help you see what the test is about and how many essays you are required to write.

2. Read each prompt carefully. Locate any key words or phrases that will help you determine the focus of the essay.

3. Note the time you have for each essay. Allow a few minutes at the beginning for prewriting. If you have time left over at the end, use it for revision. Devote the bulk of your time to writing the essay. Note: Don't stop writing to revise. It is more important to finish your essay than to revise what's already there.

4. Once you've determined the focus of the essay, organize your thoughts about the topic. Use graphic organizers if they help you get your thoughts down quickly. Then begin writing.

5. If you feel nervous before the test, try this: Close your eyes and take several slow, deep breaths. Spend a few minutes purposely trying to relax your mind.